GREEN DAY.

PRESENTS

american idiot

Special thanks to Rob Cavallo

Transcribed by Hemme Luttjeboer

Project Manager: Aaron Stang
Music Editors: Colgan Bryan & Aaron Stang
Album Art: © 2004 Reprise Records
Art Direction and Design: Chris Bilheimer
Book Art Layout: Joe Klucar

CONTENTS

⊕AMERICAN IDIOT FEB 23

1. DON'T WANT TO BE AN AMERICAN IDIOT
DON'T WANT A NATION UNDER THE NEW MANIA
CAN YOU HEAR THE SOUND OF HYSTERIA?
THE SUBLIMINAL MIND FUCK AMERICA
WELCOME TO A NEW KIND OF TENSION
ALL ACROSS THE ALIENATION
WHERE EVERYTHING ISN'T MEANT TO BE O.K.
TELEVISION DREAMS OF TOMORROW
→ WE'RE NOT THE ONES MEANT TO FOLLOW
FOR TAHAT'S ENOUGH TO ARGUE
MAYBE I AM THE FAGGOT AMERICA
I'M NOT A PART OF A REDNECK AGENDA
→ NOW EVERYBODY DO THE PROPAGANDA!
AND SING ALONG TO THE AGE OF PARANOIA
DON'T WANT TO BE AN AMERICAN IDIOT
ONE NATION ~~CONTOROLLED BY~~ THE ~~~~ MEDIA
→ INFORMATION AGE OF HYSTERIA
CALLING OUT TO IDIOT AMERICA™

②JESUS OF SUBURBIA   MAR.3   JINGLETOWN USA

I.   I'M THE SON OF RAGE AND LOVE
THE JESUS OF SUBURBIA
FROM THE BIBLE OF "NONE OF THE ABOVE"
ON A STEADY DIET OF SODA POP AND RITALIN
NO ONE EVER DIED FOR MY SINS IN HELL
AS FAR AS I CAN TELL →

AT LEAST THE ONES I GOT AWAY WITH
BUT THERE'S NOTHING WRONG WITH ME
THIS IS HOW I'M SUPPOSED TO BE
→ IN THE LAND OF MAKE BELIEVE
THAT DON'T BELIEVE IN ME
GET MY TELEVISION FIX SITTING ON MY CRUCIFIX
THE LIVING ROOM IN MY PRIVATE WOMB
WHILE THE MOM'S & BRAD'S ARE AWAY
TO FALL IN LOVE AND FALL IN DEBT
TO ALCOHOL AND CIGARETTES AND MARY JANE
TO KEEP ME INSANE AND DOING SOMEONE ELSE'S COCAINE

II. CITY OF THE DAMNED
AT THE ~~CENTER OF THE EARTH~~
IN THE PARKING LOT OF THE 7-11 WHERE I WAS TAUGHT
THE MOTTO WAS JUST A LIE
IT SAYS "HOME IS WHERE YOUR HEART IS"
BUT WHAT A SHAME
'CAUSE EVERYONE'S HEART DOESN'T BEAT THE SAME
WE'RE BEATING OUT OF TIME
CITY OF THE DEAD
AT THE END OF ANOTHER LOST HIGHWAY
SIGNS MISLEADING TO NOWHERE - CITY OF THE DAMNED
LOST CHILDREN WITH DIRTY FACES TODAY
NO ONE REALLY SEEMS TO CARE
I READ THE GRAFFITI ~~~~ IN THE BATHROOM STALL
LIKE THE HOLY SCRIPTURES IN A SHOPPING MALL
AND SO IT SEEMED TO CONFESS IT DIDN'T SAY MUCH

BUT IT ONLY CONFIRMED THAT.
THE ~~CENTER OF THE EARTH~~ IS THE ~~END OF THE WORLD~~
AND I COULD REALLY CARE LESS

III. **I DON'T CARE** I DON'T CARE
IF YOU DON'T. I DON'T CARE IF YOU
DON'T. I DON'T CARE IF YOU
DON'T CARE. EVERYONE IS SO
FULL OF ~~SHIT~~! BORN AND
RAISED BY HYPOCRITES. HEARTS
RECYCLED BUT NEVER SAVED. FROM
THE CRADLE TO THE GRAVE. WE ARE THE
KIDS OF WAR AND PEACE. FROM ANAHEIM
TO THE MIDDLE EAST. WE ARE THE STORIES
AND DISCIPLES OF THE JESUS OF
SUBURBIA, LAND OF MAKE BELIEVE
AND IT DON'T BELIEVE IN ME AND
I DON'T CARE!

IV. Dearly Beloved
DEARLY BELOVED, ARE YOU LISTENING?
I CAN'T REMEMBER A WORD THAT YOU WERE SAYING
              ARE WE DEMENTED?
          OR AM I DISTURBED?
THE SPACE THAT'S IN BETWEEN INSANE AND INSECURE
OH THERAPY, CAN YOU PLEASE FILL THE VOID?
          AM I RETARDED?
          OR AM I JUST OVERJOYED?
NOBODY'S PERFECT AND I STAND ACCUSED
FOR LACK OF A BETTER WORD AND THAT'S MY BEST EXCUSE

V. TALES OF ANOTHER BROKEN HOME
    TO LIVE AND NOT TO BREATHE
IS TO DIE IN TRAGEDY
    TO RUN, TO RUN AWAY TO FIND WHAT TO BELIEVE
    AND I LEAVE BEHIND THIS HURRICANE OF FUCKING LIES
    I LOST MY FAITH TO THIS, THIS TOWN THAT DON'T EXIST
    SO I RUN, I RUN AWAY
TO THE LIGHT OF MASOCHISTS
AND I LEAVE BEHIND THIS HURRICANE OF FUCKING LIES
AND I WALKED THIS LINE A MILLION AND ONE FUCKING TIMES
BUT NOT THIS TIME
i don't feel any shame, i won't apologize
WHEN THERE AIN'T NOWHERE YOU CAN GO
RUNNING AWAY FROM PAIN WHEN YOU'VE BEEN VICTIMIZED

TALES FROM ANOTHER BROKEN HOME

#3. HOLIDAY — APRIL 1st ~~in~~ IN THE CITY

HEAR THE SOUND OF THE FALLING RAIN.
COMING DOWN LIKE AN ARMAGEDDON FLAME
THE SHAME
THE ONES WHO DIED WITHOUT A NAME
HEAR THE DOGS HOWLING OUT OF KEY
TO A HYMN CALLED "FAITH AND MISERY" ~~ANOTHER~~
AND BLEED THE COMPANY LOST THE WAR TODAY

☆ I BEG TO DREAM AND DIFFER FROM THE HOLLOW LIES
THIS IS THE DAWNING OF THE REST OF OUR LIVES
ON HOLIDAY
HEAR THE ~~DRUM~~ POUNDING OUT OF TIME
ANOTHER PROTESTER HAS CROSSED THE LINE
TO FIND THE MONEY'S ON THE OTHER SIDE
CAN I GET ANOTHER **AMEN?**
THERE'S A **FLAG** WRAPPED AROUND A SCORE OF MEN
A GAG
A **PLASTIC BAG** ON A MONUMENT

THE REPRESENTATIVE OF CALIFORNIA HAS THE FLOOR
✝ ZIEG HEIL TO THE PRESIDENT GASMAN
BOMBS AWAY IS YOUR PUNISHMENT
PULVERIZE THE EIFFEL TOWERS
WHO CRITICIZE YOUR GOVERNMENT
BANG **BANG** GOES THE BROKEN GLASS
KILL ALL THE FAGS THAT DON'T AGREE
TRIALS BY FIRE SETTING FIRE
IS NOT A WAY THAT'S MEANT FOR ME

JUSTCAUSE — JUST CAUSE BECAUSE WE'RE **OUTLAWS** YEAH!
I BEG TO DREAM AND DIFFER FROM THE HOLLOW LIES
THIS IS THE DAWNING OF THE REST OF OUR LIVES
THIS IS OUR LIVES ON HOLIDAY

4. **BOULEVARD OF BROKEN DREAMS** BLVD

APRIL 2 I WALK A LONELY ROAD
THE ONLY ONE THAT I HAVE EVER KNOWN
DON'T KNOW WHERE IT GOES
BUT IT'S HOME TO ME AND I WALK ALONE
~~WHERE~~ I WALK THIS EMPTY STREET
ON THE BLVD. OF BROKEN DREAMS
WHERE THE CITY SLEEPS
AND I'M THE ONLY ONE AND I WALK ALONE
I WALK ALONE. I WALK ALONE. I WALK ALONE. I WALK ALONE.
MY SHADOW'S THE ONLY ONE THAT WALKS BESIDE ME
MY SHALLOW HEART'S THE ONLY THING ~~THAT~~ THAT'S BEATING
SOMETIMES I WISH SOMEONE OUT THERE WILL FIND ME
'TIL THEN I WALK ALONE
I'M WALKING DOWN THE LINE
THAT DIVIDES ME SOMEWHERE IN MY MIND
ON THE BORDERLINE OF THE EDGE
AND WHERE I WALK ALONE
READ ~~BETWEEN~~ THE LINES OF WHAT'S
FUCKED UP AND EVERYTHING'S ALRIGHT
CHECK MY VITAL SIGNS TO KNOW I'M STILL ALIVE

AND I WALK ALONE

I WALK ALONE. I WALK ALONE. I WALK ALONE. I WALK ALONE
I WALK THIS EMPTY STREET ON THE BLVD. OF BROKEN DREAMS
WHERE THE CITY SLEEPS
AND I'M THE ONLY ONE AND I WALK ALONE
MY SHADOW'S THE ONLY ONE THAT WALKS BESIDE ME
MY SHALLOW HEART'S THE ONLY THING THAT'S BEATING
SOMETIMES I WISH SOMEONE OUT THERE WILL FIND ME
'TIL THEN, I WALK ALONE

5. Are We The Waiting

EASTER SUNDAY

STARRY NIGHTS CITY LIGHTS
COMING DOWN OVER ME
SKY SCRAPERS AND STARGAZERS IN MY HEAD
ARE WE WE ARE, ARE WE WE ARE THE WAITING UNKNOWN
THIS DIRTY TOWN WAS BURNING DOWN IN MY DREAMS
LOST AND FOUND CITY BOUND IN MY DREAMS & **SCREAMING**
ARE WE WE ARE, ARE WE WE ARE THE WAITING AND
SCREAMING ARE WE WE ARE ARE WE WE ARE THE WAITING
FOR GET ME NOTS AND SECOND THOUGHTS
LIVE IN ISOLATION
HEADS OR TAILS AND FAIRYTALES IN MY MIND
ARE WE WE ARE, ARE WE WE ARE THE WAITING UNKNOWN
THE **RAGE AND LOVE**, THE STORY OF MY LIFE
THE **JESUS OF SUBURBIA** IS A LIE & SCREAMING
ARE WE WE ARE, ARE WE WE ARE THE WAITING UNKNOWN
ARE WE WE ARE, ARE WE WE ARE THE WAITING UNKNOWN
ARE WE WE ARE, ARE WE WE ARE THE WAITING UNKNOWN
ARE WE WE ARE, ARE WE WE ARE THE WAITING UNKNOWN

ARE WE WE ARE ~~ARE~~ WE WE ARE THE WAITING UNKNOWN

6. St. Jimmy

MAY 7

ST. JIMMY'S COMING DOWN ACROSS THE ALLEYWAY
UPON THE BLVD. LIKE A ZIP GUN ON PARADE
LIGHT OF A SILHOUETTE, HE'S INSUBORDINATE
COMING AT YOU ON THE COUNT OF **1, 2, 3, 4**
MY NAME IS JIMMY AND YOU BETTER NOT WEAR IT OUT.
SUICIDE COMMANDO THAT YOUR MOMMA TALKED ABOUT. KING
OF THE 40 THIEVES AND I'M HERE TO REPRESENT THE
NEEDLE IN THE VEIN OF THE ESTABLISHMENT. I'M THE
PATRON SAINT OF THE DENIAL WITH AN **ANGEL FACE** AND
A TASTE FOR SUICIDAL CIGARETTES AND RAMEN AND A
LITTLE BAG OF DOPE. I AM THE SON OF A BITCH AND EDGAR
ALLAN POE. RAISED IN THE CITY UNDER A HALO OF LIGHTS.
THE PRODUCT OF WAR AND FEAR THAT WE'VE BEEN VICTIMIZED.
ARE YOU TALKING TO ME? MY NAME IS ST. JIMMY. I'M A
SON OF A GUN. I'M THE ONE THAT'S FROM THE WAY OUTSIDE.
I'M A TEENAGE ASSASSIN EXECUTING SOME FUN IN THE CULT
OF THE LIFE OF CRIME. I'D REALLY HATE TO SAY IT, BUT I
TOLD YOU SO. SO SHUT YOUR MOUTH BEFORE I SHOOT YOU DOWN
OL' BOY. WELCOME TO THE CLUB AND GIVE ME SOME BLOOD.
I'M THE RESIDENT LEADER OF THE LOST AND FOUND. IT'S COMEDY
AND TRAGEDY. IT'S ST. JIMMY, AND THAT'S MY NAME
AND DON'T WEAR IT OUT

7. GIVE ME NOVACAINE

JUNE 13

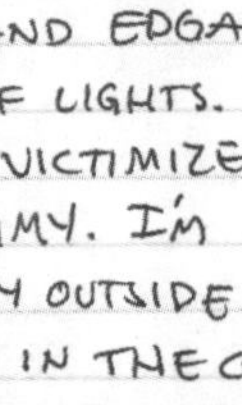

TAKE AWAY THE SENSATION INSIDE
BITTERSWEET MIGRAINE IN MY HEAD

IT'S LIKE A THROBBING TOOTHACHE OF THE MIND
I CAN'T TAKE THIS FEELING ANY MORE
DRAIN THE PRESSURE FROM THE SWELLING
THIS SENSATION'S OVER WHELMING
GIVE ME A LONG KISS GOODNIGHT
AND EVERYTHING WILL BE ALRIGHT
TELL ME THAT I WON'T FEEL A THING
GIVE ME NOVACAINE
OUT OF BODY AND OUT OF MIND
KISS THE DEMONS OUT OF MY DREAMS
I GET THE FUNNY FEELING AND THAT'S ALRIGHT
JIMMY SAYS IT'S BETTER THAN HERE
DRAIN THE PRESSURE FROM THE SWELLING
THIS SENSATION'S OVER WHELMING
GIVE ME A LONG KISS GOOD NIGHT
AND EVERYTHING WILL BE ALRIGHT
TELL ME JIMMY I WON'T FEEL A THING

GIVE ME NOVA CAINE

SHE'S A REBEL		
SHE'S A REBEL	8	FROM CHICAGO / JULY 4
SHE'S A SAINT		TO TORONTO
SHE'S THE SALT OF THE EARTH		SHE'S THE ONE THAT THEY
AND SHE'S DANGEROUS		CALL OLD WHATSERNAME
SHE'S A REBEL		SHE'S THE SYMBOL
VIGILANTE		OF RESISTANCE
MISSING LINK ON THE BRINK		AND SHE'S HOLDING ON MY
OF DESTRUCTION		HEART LIKE A HANDGRENADE

IS SHE THINKING	TWIST OF FATE
WHAT I'M THINKING?	OR A MELODY THAT
IS SHE THE MOTHER OF ALL BOMBS?	SHE SINGS THE REVOLUTION
GONNA DETONATE	THE DAWNING OF OUR LIVES
IS SHE TROUBLE	SHE BRINGS THIS LIBERATION
LIKE I'M TROUBLE?	THAT I JUST CAN'T DEFINE
MAKE IT A DOUBLE	NOTHING COMES TO MIND

SHE'S AN **EXTRAORDINARY GIRL** 9
IN AN ORDINARY WORLD
AND SHE CAN'T SEEM TO GET AWAY
he lacks the courage in his mind
like a child left behind
like a pet left in the rain
SHE'S ALL ALONE AGAIN
WIPING THE TEARS FROM HER EYES
Some days he feels like dying
SHE GETS SO SICK OF CRYING
SHE SEES THE MIRROR OF HERSELF
AN IMAGE SHE WANTS TO SELL
TO ANYONE WILLING TO BUY
he steals the image in her kiss
from her heart's apocalypse
from the one called whatsername

SHE'S ALL ALONE AGAIN
WIPING THE TEARS FROM HER EYES
Some days he feels like dying
Some days it's not worth trying
now that they both are finding
SHE GETS SO SICK OF CRYING

Dear J,

Where have all the bastards gone? The underbelly stacks up ten high. The dummy failed the crash test, now collecting unemployment checks like a flunkie along for the ride.

Where have all the riots gone as the city's motto gets pulverized?

"What's in love is now in debt" on your birth certificate. So strike the fucking match to light this fuse! The town bishop is an extortionist and he don't even know that you exist. Standing still when it's do or die, you better run for your fucking life. It's not over till you're underground. It's not over before it's too late. This city's burning "It's not my burden". It's not over before it's too late; there is nothing left to analyze. Where will all the martyrs go when the virus cures itself? And where will we all go when it's too late?

You're not the Jesus of Suburbia

The St. Jimmy is a figment of your father's rage and your mother's love. —W

Aug. 18th

LETTER BOMB
10

MADE ME THE IDIOT AMERICA. It's not over 'til you're underground. It's not over before it's too late. This city's burning. "It's not my burden." It's not over before it's too late. She said "I can't take this place." I'm leaving it behind. She said "I can't take this town, I'm leaving you tonight."

Sept. 10
11.

(WAKE ME UP WHEN SEPTEMBER ENDS)

SUMMER HAS COME AND PASSED
THE INNOCENT CAN NEVER LAST
WAKE ME UP WHEN SEPTEMBER ENDS
LIKE MY FATHER'S COME TO PASS
SEVEN YEARS HAS GONE SO FAST
WAKE ME UP WHEN SEPTEMBER ENDS
HERE COMES THE RAIN AGAIN
FALLING FROM THE STARS
DRENCHED IN MY PAIN AGAIN
BECOMING WHO WE ARE
AS MY MEMORY RESTS
BUT NEVER FORGETS ~~WHAT I LOST~~
WAKE ME UP WHEN SEPTEMBER ENDS
SUMMER HAS COME AND PASSED
THE INNOCENT CAN NEVER LAST
WAKE ME ~~UP~~ UP WHEN SEPTEMBER ENDS
RING OUT THE BELLS AGAIN
LIKE WE DID WHEN SPRING BEGAN
WAKE ME UP WHEN SEPTEMBER ENDS
HERE COMES THE RAIN AGAIN
FALLING FROM THE STARS
DRENCHED IN MY PAIN AGAIN
BECOMING WHO WE ARE
AS MY MEMORY RESTS
BUT NEVER FORGETS WHAT I LOST
WAKE ME UP WHEN SEPTEMBER ENDS

SUMMER HAS COME AND PASSED, THE INNOCENT CAN NEVER LAST
WAKE ME UP WHEN SEPTEMBER ENDS
LIKE MY FATHER'S COME TO PASS, TWENTY YEARS HAS GONE SO FAST

WAKE ME UP WHEN SEPTEMBER ENDS

12 HOMECOMING

I. THE DEATH OF ST. JIMMY

MY HEART IS BEATING FROM ME
I AM STANDING ALL ALONE. PLEASE CALL ME
ONLY IF YOU ARE COMING HOME
WASTE ANOTHER YEAR FLIES BY **WASTE** A NIGHT OR TWO
YOU TAUGHT ME HOW TO LIVE IN THE STREETS OF SHAME
WHERE YOU'VE LOST YOUR DREAMS IN THE RAIN
THERE'S NO SIGN OF HOPE
THE STEMS AND SEEDS OF THE LAST OF THE DOPE
THERE'S A GLOW OF LIGHT. THE **ST. JIMMY** IS THE SPARK IN THE NIGHT
BEARING GIFTS AND TRUST. THE FIXTURE IN THE CITY OF LUST.
"WHAT THE HELL'S YOUR NAME?"
WHAT'S YOUR PLEASURE AND WHAT'S YOUR PAIN?
DO YOU DREAM TOO MUCH?
DO YOU THINK WHAT YOU NEED IS A CRUTCH?
IN THE CROWD OF PAIN, ST. JIMMY COMES WITHOUT ANY SHAME
HE SAYS "WE'RE FUCKED UP"
BUT WE'RE NOT THE SAME
AND MOM AND DAD ARE THE ONES YOU CAN BLAME

> JIMMY DIED TODAY.

HE BLEW HIS BRAINS OUT INTO THE BAY
IN THE STATE OF MIND
IN MY OWN PRIVATE SUICIDE

II. EAST 12TH ST. AND ~~NOBODY CARES~~
AND NOBODY CARES

DOES ANYONE CARE IF NOBODY CARES?
AND NOBODY CARES AND NOBODY CARES
DOES ANYONE CARE IF NOBODY CARES?
JESUS FILLING OUT PAPERWORK NOW
AT THE FACILITY ON EAST 12TH ST
HE'S NOT LISTENING TO A WORD NOW
HE'S IN HIS OWN WORLD AND HE'S DAYDREAMING
HE'D RATHER BE DOING SOMETHING ELSE NOW
LIKE CIGARETTES AND COFFEE WITH THE **UNDERBELLY**
HIS LIFE ON THE LINE WITH ANXIETY NOW
AND ~~SHE~~ HAD ENOUGH
AND ~~HE'S~~ HAD PLENTY
SOMEBODY GET ME OUT OF HERE
ANYBODY GET ME OUT OF HERE
SOMEBODY GET ME OUT OF HERE
GET ME THE FUCK RIGHT OUT OF HERE
SO FAR AWAY, I DON'T WANT TO STAY
GET ME OUTTA HERE RIGHT NOW
I JUST WANT TO BE FREE
IS THERE A POSSIBILITY?
GET ME OUT OF HERE RIGHT NOW
THIS LIFELIKE DREAM AIN'T FOR ME

III. NOBODY LIKES YOU! NOV 10

I FELL ASLEEP WHILE WATCHING SPIKE TV AFTER 10 CUP'S OF COFFEE AND YOU'RE STILL <u>NOT HERE</u>. DREAMING OF A SONG WHEN SOMETHING WENT WRONG, BUT I CAN'T TELL ANYONE 'CUZ YOU'RE NOT HERE. **LEFT ME HERE ALONE WHEN I SHOULDHAVE STAYED HOME** AFTER 10 CUPS OF COFFEE I'M THINKING. WHERE'D YOU GO?
NOBODY LIKES YOU EVERYONE LEFT YOU
THEY'RE ALL OUT WITHOUT YOU HAVIN' FUN
EVERYONE LEFT YOU NOBODY LIKES YOU
THEY'RE ALL OUT WITHOUT YOU, HAVIN' FUN
WHERE'D YOU GO?

DEAR J.

I got a Rock and Roll band
I got a Rock and Roll life
I got a Rock and Roll girlfriend
AND ANOTHER EX-WIFE
I got a Rock AND Roll house
I got a Rock AND Roll CAR

I play the shit out the DRUMS
AND I CAN PLAY THE GUITAR
I GOT A KID IN NEW YORK
I GOT A KID IN THE BAY
I HAVEN'T DRANK OR SMOKED NOTHIN'
IN OVER 22 DAYS
SO GET OFF OF MY CASE
                    — Tunny

SAINT JIMMY

V.

<u>WE'RE COMING HOME AGAIN</u>

HERE THEY COME MARCHING DOWN THE STREET
LIKE A DESPERATION MURMUR OF A HEART BEAT
COMING BACK FROM THE EDGE OF TOWN
UNDERNEATH THEIR FEET, THE TIME HAS COME
AND IT'S GOING NOWHERE
NOBODY EVER SAID THAT LIFE WAS FAIR NOW
GO-CARTS AND GUNS ARE TREASURES THEY WILL BEAR
IN THE SUMMER HEAT
THE WORLD IS SPINNING AROUND AND AROUND
OUT OF CONTROL AGAIN
FROM THE 7-11 TO THE FEAR OF BREAKING DOWN
SO SEND MY LOVE A LETTERBOMB
AND VISIT ME IN HELL
WE'RE THE ONES GOING HOME
WE'RE COMING HOME AGAIN

I STARTED FUCKIN' RUNNING
JUST AS SOON AS MY FEET TOUCH GROUND
WE'RE BACK IN THE BARRIO
BUT TO YOU AND ME, THAT'S JINGLE TOWN
  HOME.
    WE'RE COMING HOME AGAIN   HAVIN' FUN!
NOBODY LIKES YOU - EVERYONE LEFT YOU - THEY'RE ALL OUT WITHOUT YOU

THOUGHT I RAN INTO YOU DOWN ON THE STREET
THEN IT TURNED OUT TO ONLY BE A DREAM
I MADE A POINT TO BURN ALL OF THE PHOTOGRAPHS
SHE WENT AWAY AND THEN I TOOK A DIFFERENT PATH
I CAN REMEMBER THE FACE, BUT I CAN'T RECALL THE NAME
NOW I WONDER HOW ~~WHATSERNAME~~ HAS BEEN
SEEMS THAT SHE DISAPPEARED WITHOUT A TRACE
DID SHE MARRY OLD WHAT'S HIS FACE
I MADE A POINT TO BURN ALL OF THE PHOTOGRAPHS
SHE WENT AWAY AND THEN I TOOK A DIFFERENT PATH
I REMEMBER THE FACE, BUT I CAN'T RECALL THE NAME
NOW I WONDER HOW ~~WHATSERNAME~~ HAS BEEN
REMEMBER, WHATEVER
IT SEEMS LIKE FOREVER AGO
REMEMBER, WHATEVER
IT SEEMS LIKE FOREVER AGO
THE REGRETS ARE USELESS, IN MY MIND
~~━━━━━━━~~ SHE'S IN MY HEAD
I MUST CONFESS, THE REGRETS ARE USELESS
~~━━━━━━~~ SHE'S IN MY HEAD
FROM SO LONG AGO AND IN THE DARKEST NIGHT
IF MY MEMORY SERVES ME RIGHT
I'LL NEVER TURN BACK TIME

FORGETTING YOU, BUT NOT THE TIME

JANUARY 1

WHATSERNAME   13.

AMERICAN IDIOT

Words by BILLIE JOE
Music by GREEN DAY

14

Verse 3:

w/Rhy. Fig. 1 (Elec. Gtr. 1)

Don't want to be an A - mer - i - can id - i - ot, one na - tion con - trolled_

18

we're   not   the   ones____   who're   meant   to   fol - low,_____

____   for   that's   e - nough____   to   ar - gue.

Outro:

Elec. Gtr. 1

Elec. Gtr. 2 enters

1.

2.

Elec. Gtr. 1

Elec. Gtr. 2 enters

JESUS OF SUBURBIA

Moderately ♩ = 144

Words by BILLIE JOE
Music by GREEN DAY

I. Jesus of Suburbia (0:00)

Verse:

*Elec. Gtr. 1 is dbld.

Interlude:

w/Rhy. Fig. 1 *(Elec. Gtr. 1)*

(Ooh._____)

Moderately slow ♩ = 72 **(half time)**

II. City of the Damned (1:51)

Acous. Gtr.

mf

1. At the

Verse:

Acous. Gtr. cont. rhy. simile

cen - ter of the earth in the park - ing lot_ of the Sev - en E - lev - en where_ I was taught_

read the graf - fi - ti in the bath - room stall_ like the Ho - ly Scrip - tures of the shop - ping mall._

Elec. Gtr. 1

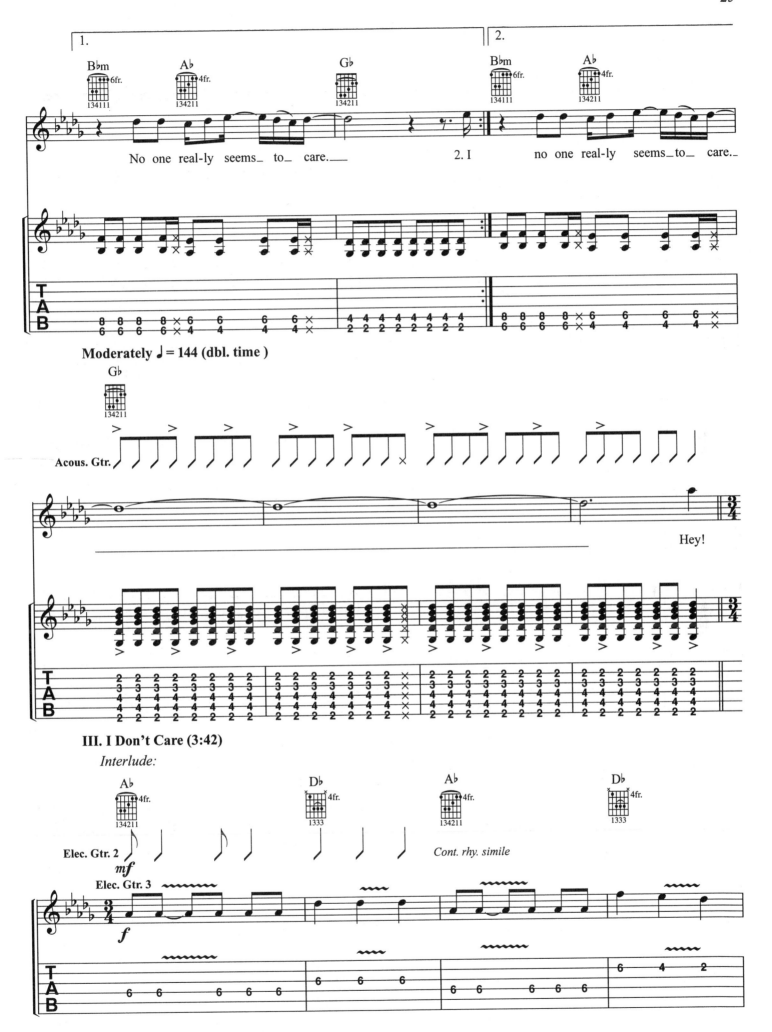

III. I Don't Care (3:42)

Interlude:

26

Chorus:

I don't care if you don't... I don't care if you don't...

I don't care if you don't care.

care. I don't care.

Verse:

Ev-'ry-one's so full of s***,__ born and raised by hy-po-crites.__

*Chord implied by bass gtr.

Jesus of Suburbia - 18 - 8
PGM0423

The space that's in__ be- tween__ in - sane and in- se - cure.__

end Rhy. Fig. 2

w/Rhy. Fig. 2 *(Elec. Gtr. 2) 4 times*

(Ooh._____)   (Ooh._____)

(Ooh.___ Oh, ther-a - py,__ can you_ please fill__ the void?_____)

(Ooh.___ Am I re-tard - ed or am I just o - ver - joyed?__)

(Ooh.___ No- bod- y's per- fect and_ I stand__ ac- cused,_____)

Moderately slow ♩ = 72 (♫=♫)

V. Tales of Another Broken Home (6:31)

Interlude:

Verse:

w/Rhy. Fig. 3 *(Elec. Gtr. 1) 7 times*

live and not to breathe is to die in trag - e -

lost my faith to this, this town that don't ex -

Rhy. Fig. 3

34

Bridge:

All Gtrs. tacet
piano & vocal only

I don't feel an-y shame,__ I won't a-pol-o-gize

when there ain't no-where you can go.__ Run-ning a-way__ from pain__ when

you've been vic-tim-ized. Tales from an-oth-er bro-ken...._____

Outro:

w/Rhy. Fig. 3 *(Elec. Gtr. 1) 4 times*

You're leav-ing, you're leav-ing,

(Home._____

you're leav - ing,   are   you leav - ing

home?

Elec. Gtr. 2

Elec. Gtr. 1

HOLIDAY

Words by BILLIE JOE
Music by GREEN DAY

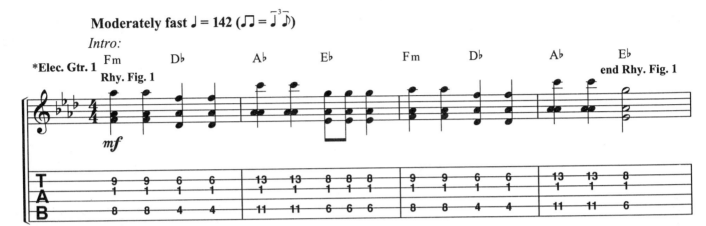

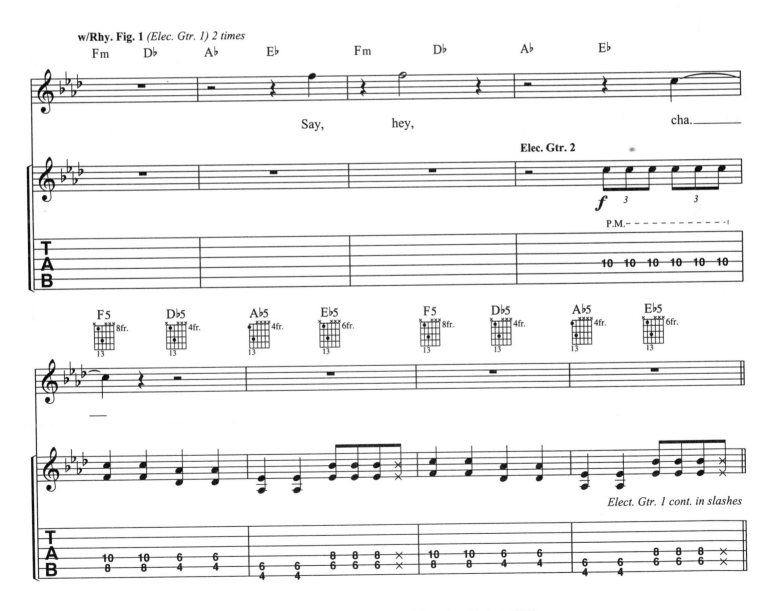

*Elec. Gtr. 1 is capoed at 1st fret but written in actual pitch. Tablature indicating 1st fret is played open with capo.

38

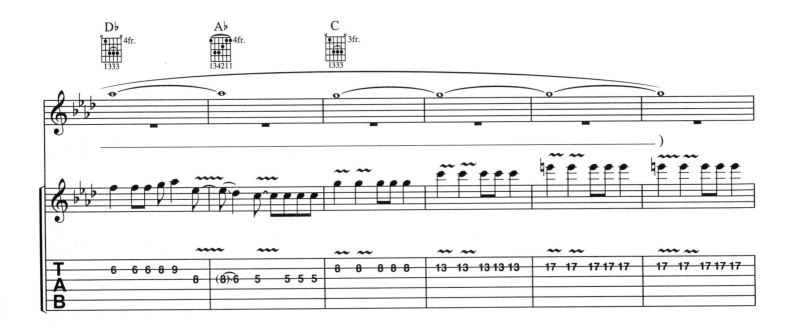

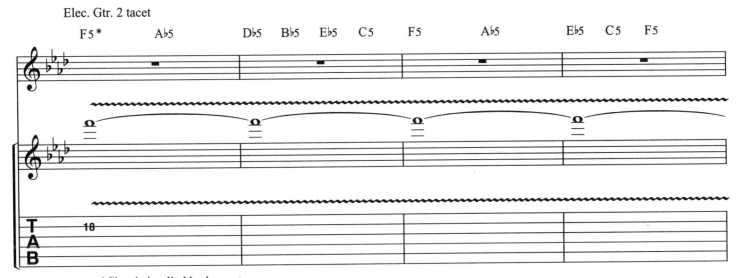

*Chords implied by bass gtr.

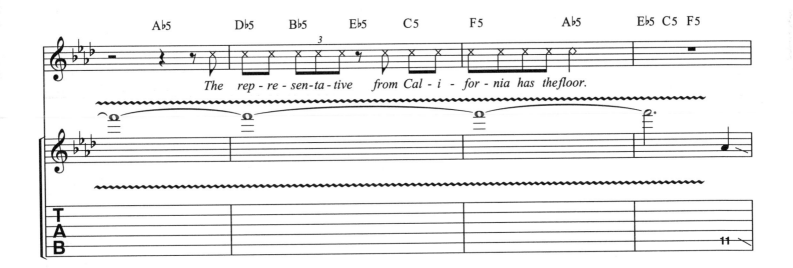

42

Holiday - 8 - 6
PGM0423

BOULEVARD OF BROKEN DREAMS

Words by BILLIE JOE
Music by GREEN DAY

*Chord is held over from previous song "Holiday."

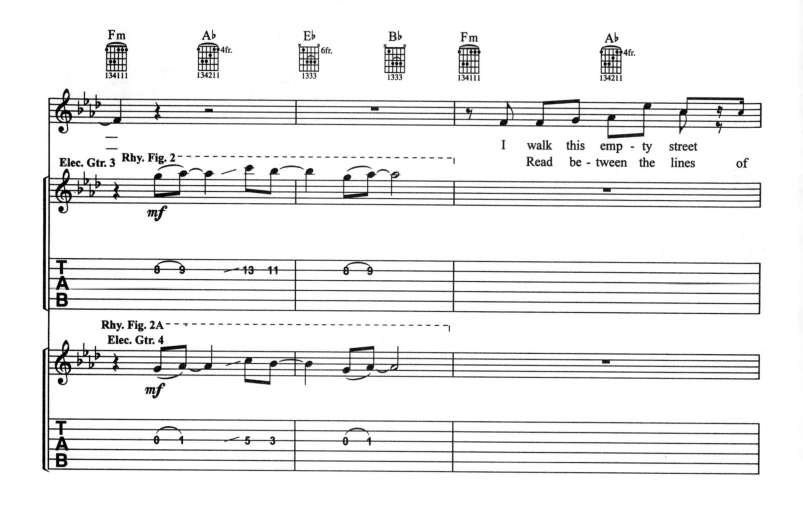

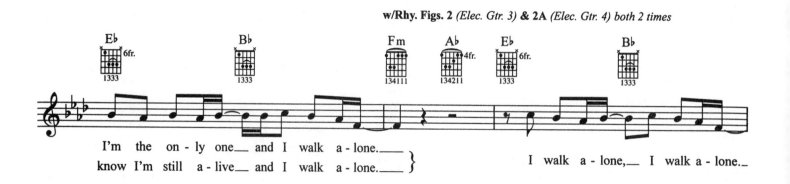

48

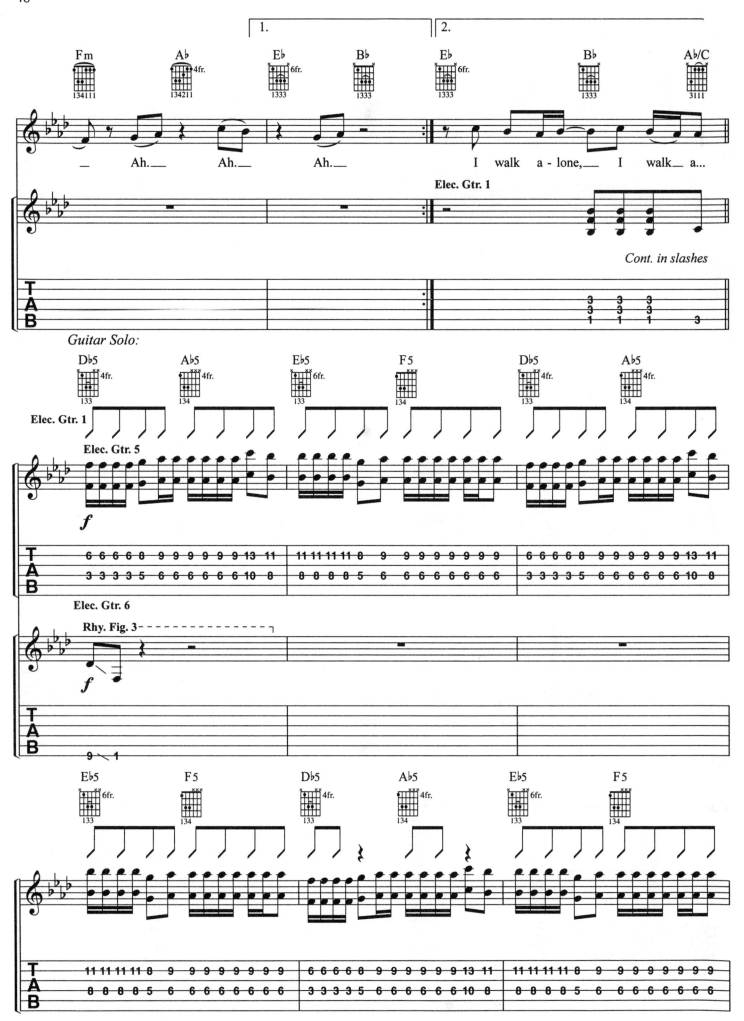

ARE WE THE WAITING

Words by BILLIE JOE
Music by GREEN DAY

Chorus:

ST. JIMMY

Words by BILLIE JOE
Music by GREEN DAY

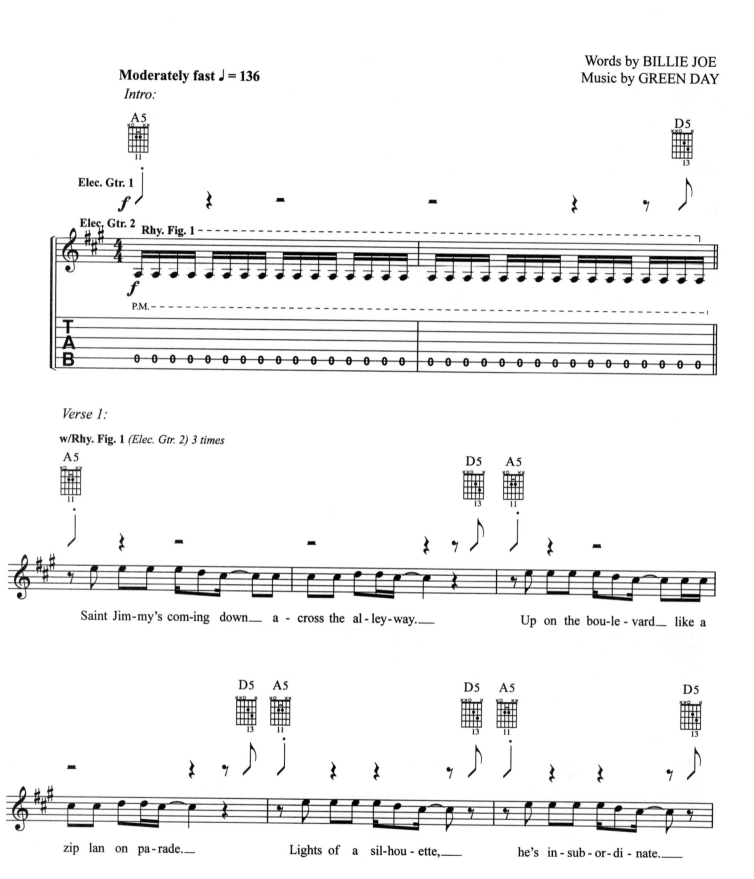

56

the need - le   in the   vein___ of   the   es - tab - lish - ment.___   I'm the
pro - duct of war and fear___ that   we've been vic - tim - ized.___ }

Pre-chorus:

Cont. rhy. simile

pa - tron   saint of the de - ni - al   with an

Elec. Gtr. 1

an - gel face and a taste   for   sui - cid - al.

Resume rhy. simile

Elec. Gtr. 1

taste   for   sui - cid - al.

Interlude:

Cont. rhy. simile

Are you talk - ing to me?___

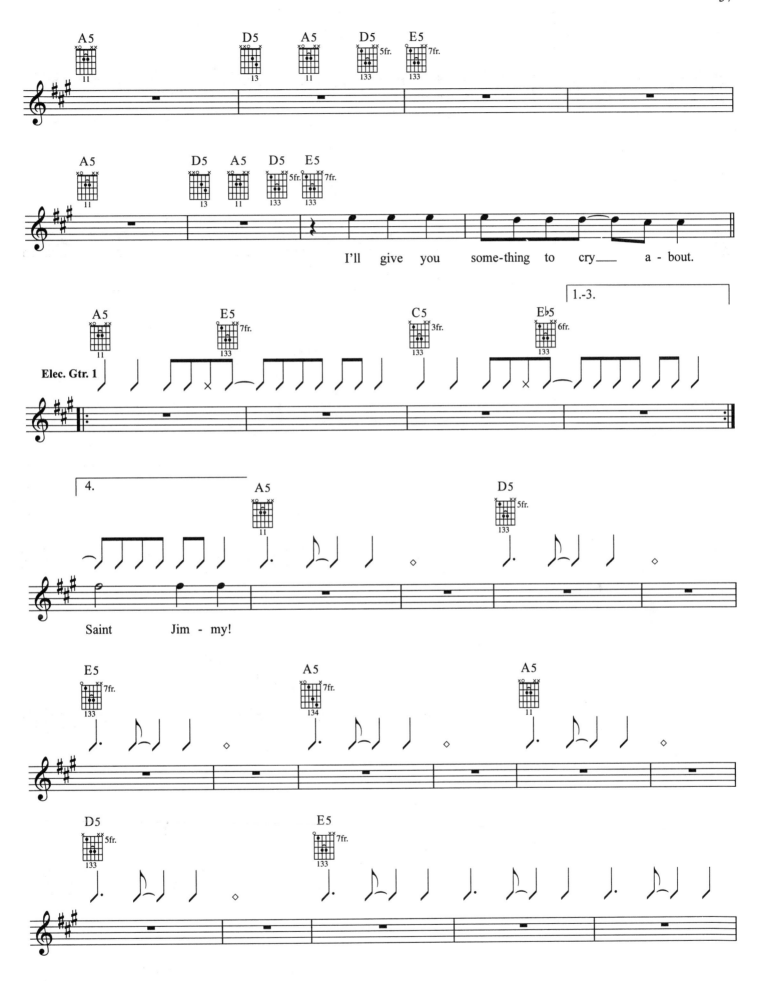

58

GIVE ME NOVACAINE

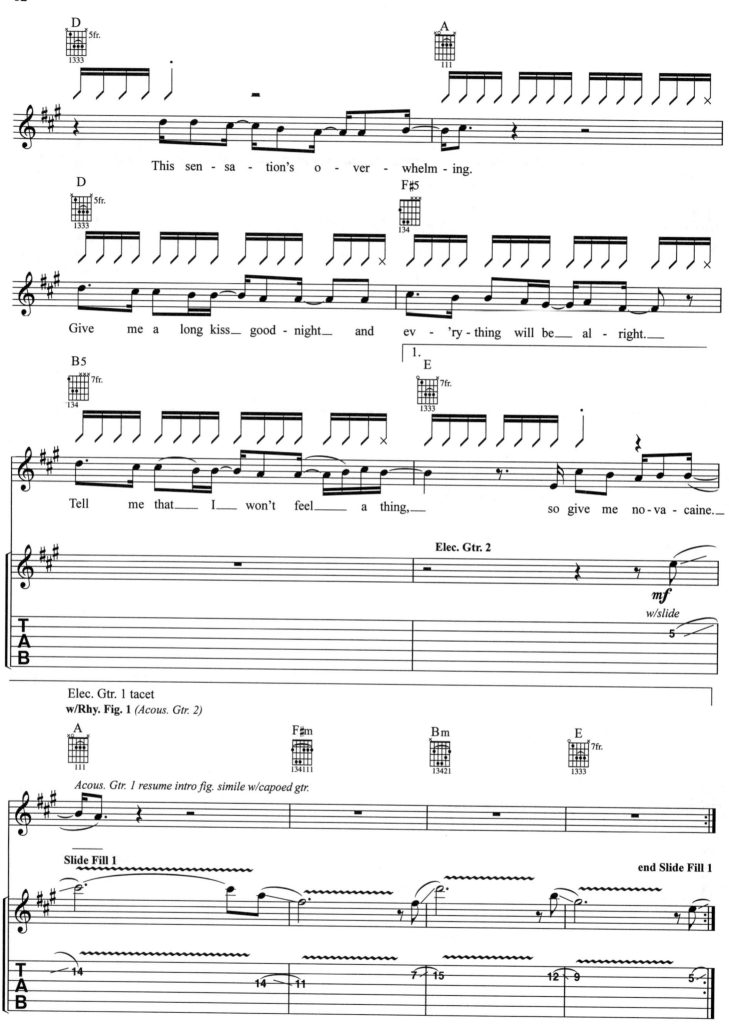

This sen - sa - tion's o - ver - whelm - ing.

Give me a long kiss__ good - night__ and ev - 'ry - thing will be__ al - right.__

Tell me that__ I__ won't feel__ a thing,__ so give me no - va - caine.

Elec. Gtr. 2

mf
w/slide

Elec. Gtr. 1 tacet
w/Rhy. Fig. 1 *(Acous. Gtr. 2)*

Acous. Gtr. 1 resume intro fig. simile w/capoed gtr.

Slide Fill 1

end Slide Fill 1

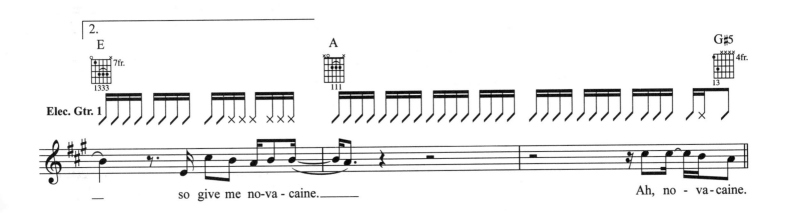

so give me no-va-caine._____

Ah, no - va - caine.

Guitar Solo:

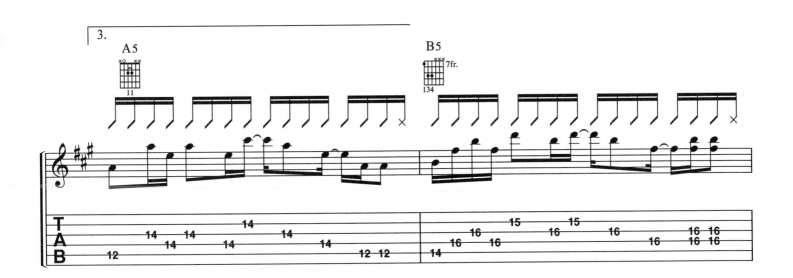

SHE'S A REBEL

Moderately fast ♩ = 148

Words by BILLIE JOE
Music by GREEN DAY

Chorus:

She's a reb - el, she's a saint,_____ she's the salt of the earth and she's dan - ger - ous.____ She's a reb - el, vig - i - lan - te,____

Verse:

miss-ing link on the brink of de - struc - tion.____ 1. From Chi - ca - go 2. Is she dream - ing to To - ron - to,____ she's the one that they call "old what's-'er - name."__ what I'm think - ing.____ Is she the moth - er of all bombs gon - na det - o - nate?____

EXTRAORDINARY GIRL

Words by BILLIE JOE
Music by GREEN DAY

Moderately ♩ = 112

Intro:

Faster ♩ = 142

band enters

Elec. Sitar
Rhy. Fig. 1A

end Rhy. Fig. 1A

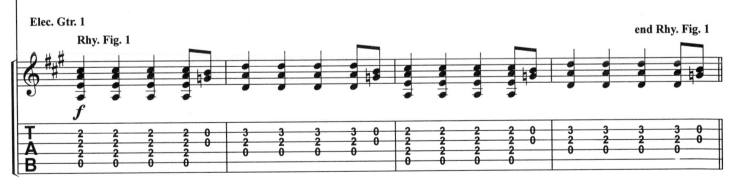

Elec. Gtr. 1
Rhy. Fig. 1

end Rhy. Fig. 1

70

Verse:

72

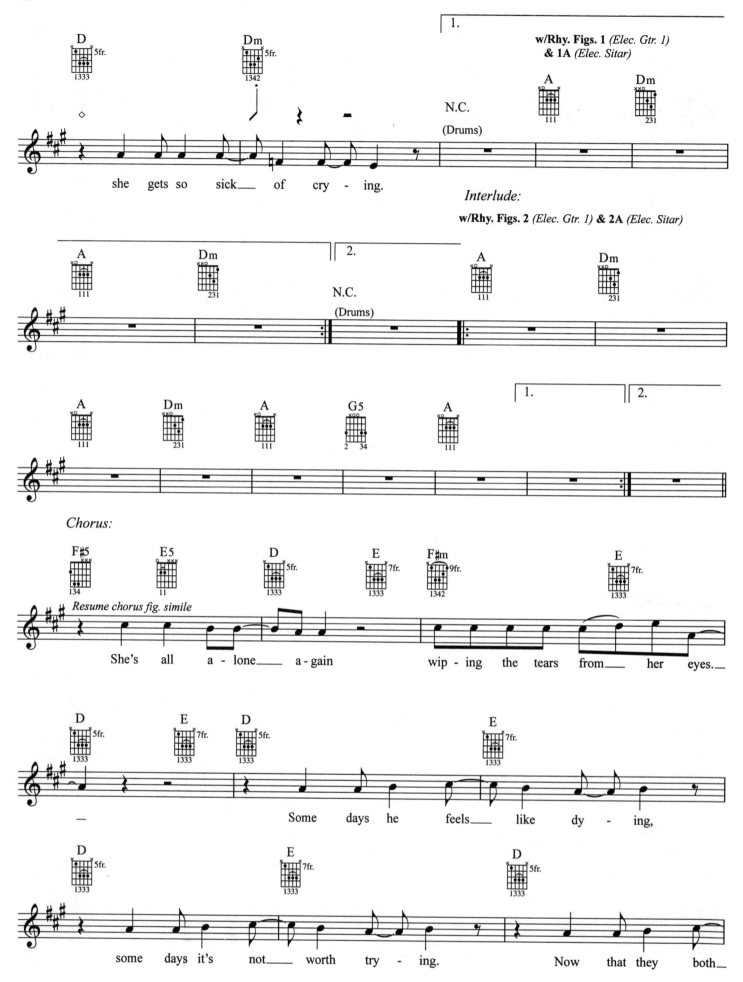

LETTER BOMB

Words by BILLIE JOE
Music by GREEN DAY

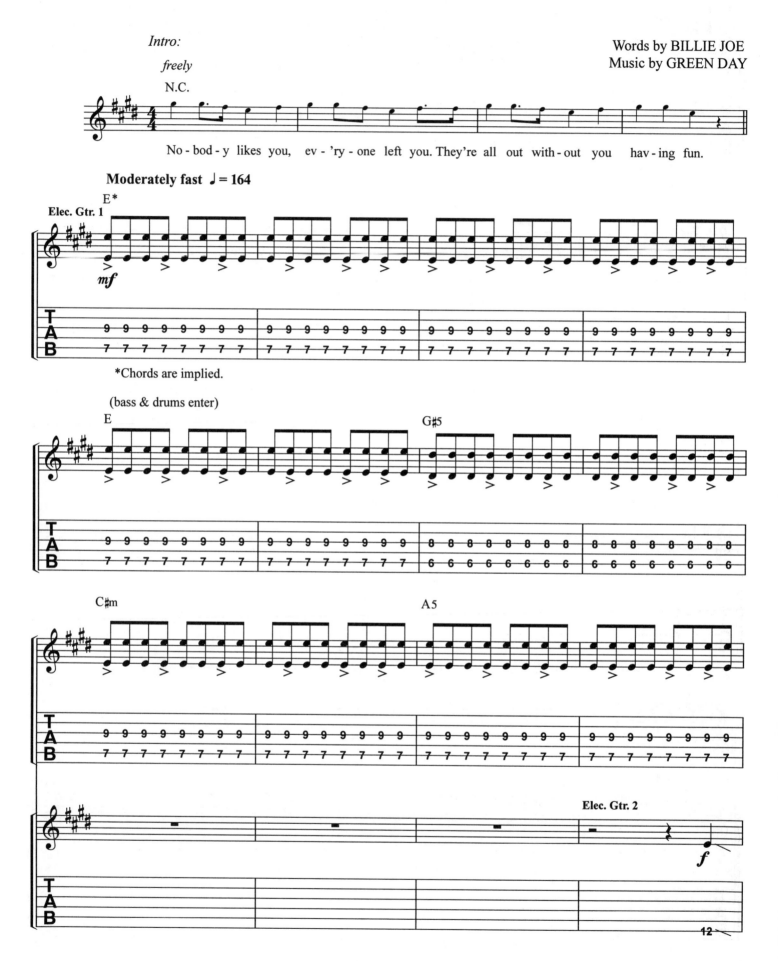

*Chords are implied.

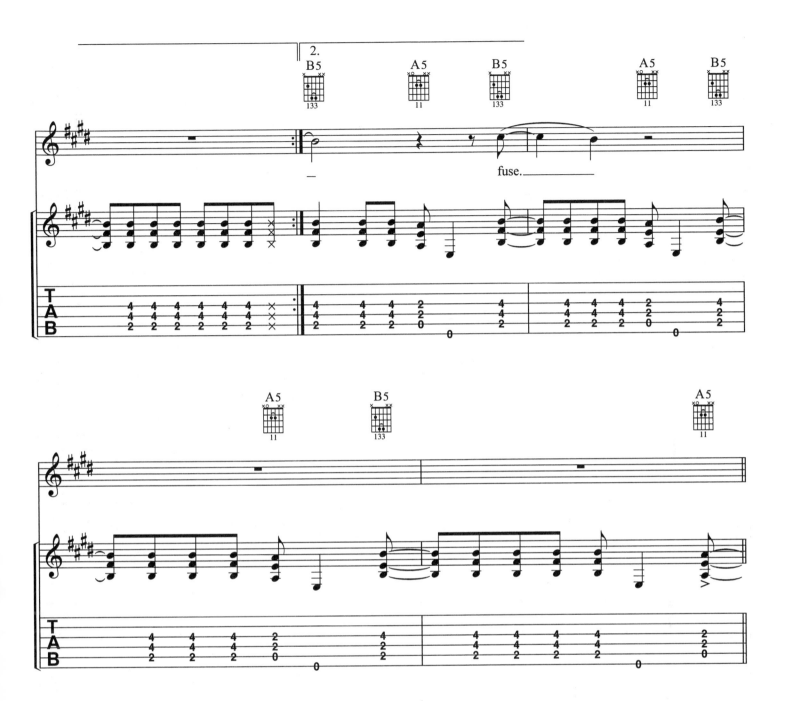

Pre-chorus:

The town bish-op's an ex - tor-tion-ist,   and he don't e - ven know that

78

Chorus:

Letter Bomb - 11 - 5
PGM0423

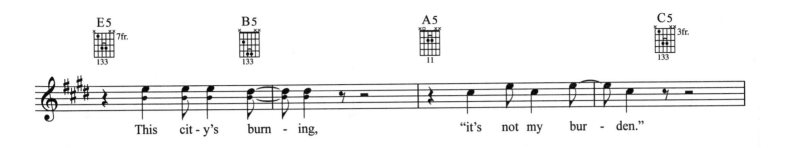

This cit - y's burn - ing, "it's not my bur - den."

It's not o - ver be - fore__ it's too late.

Elec. Gtr. 2

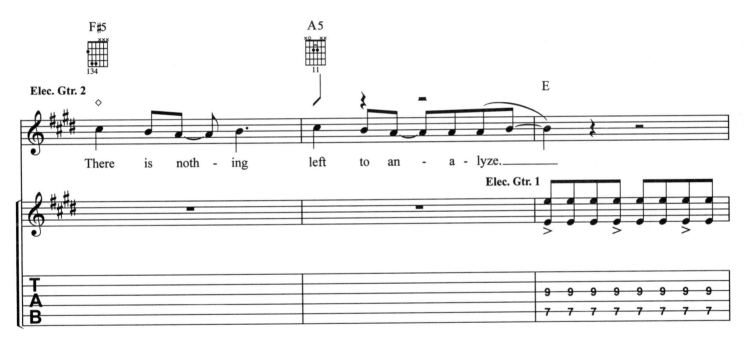

There is noth - ing left to an - a - lyze.__

Elec. Gtr. 1

80

Midtro:

84

WAKE ME UP WHEN SEPTEMBER ENDS

Words by BILLIE JOE
Music by GREEN DAY

86

Verse 3:

Sum - mer— has come and passed,— the in - no - cent— can nev-

- er last._____ Wake me up—— when Sep - tem - ber ends.—

90

Chorus:

Verse 4:

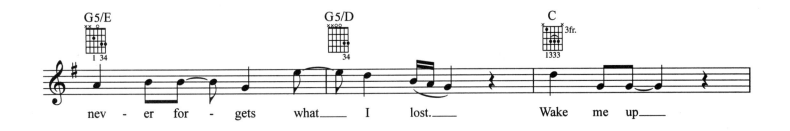

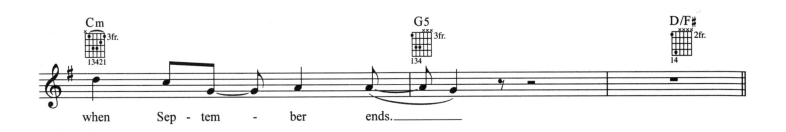

92

Guitar Solo:

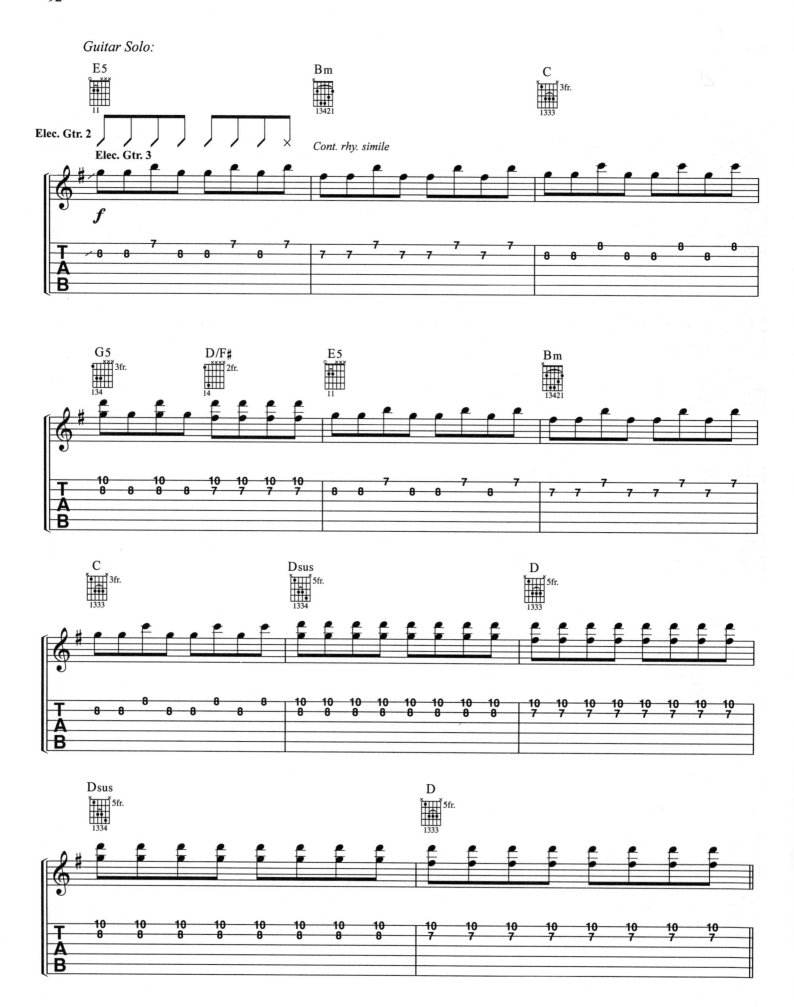

Interlude:

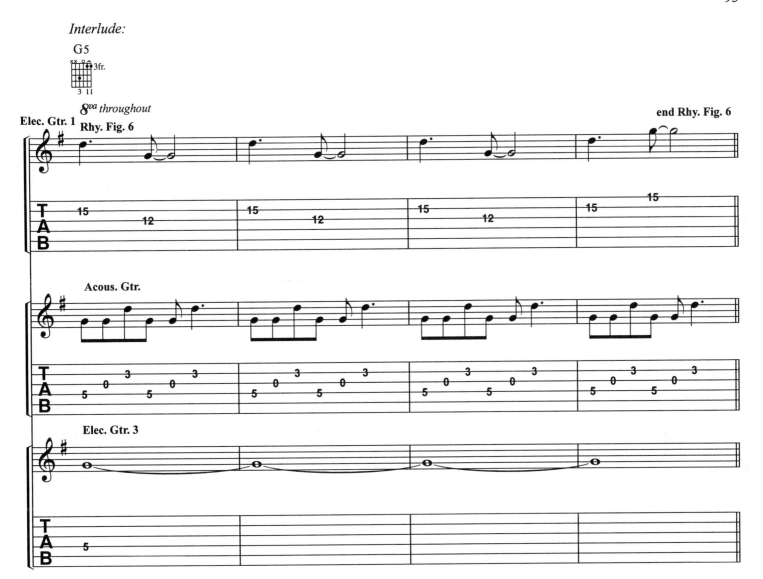

Verse 5:

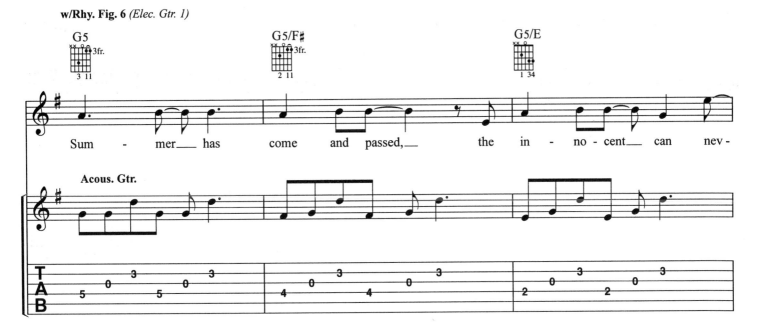

Sum - mer __ has come and passed, __ the in - no - cent __ can nev-

94

HOMECOMING

Words by BILLIE JOE
Music by GREEN DAY

Moderately ♩ = 120

I. The Death of St. Jimmy (0:00)

Intro:

Verse 1:

Elec. Gtr. 1 cont. rhy. simile

My heart___ is beat-ing from___me, I am stand - ing___ all a - lone.___

Please___ call___ me___ on - ly if you___ are___ com - ing home.___

Waste an-oth-er year___ flies___ by,___ waste a night or two.___

Elec. Gtr. 1

* Elec. Gtr. 2 dbld. by Acous. Gtr.

98

II. East 12th St. (2:25)

Words by BILLIE JOE
Music by GREEN DAY

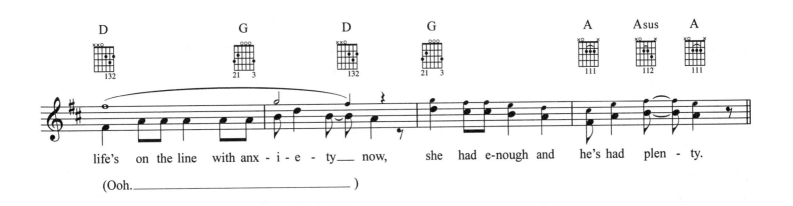

life's on the line with anx - i - e - ty___ now, she had e-nough and he's had plen - ty.

(Ooh._____)

Bridge:

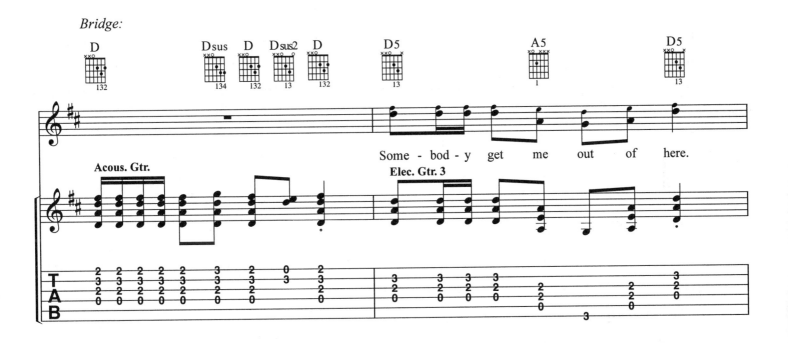

Some - bod - y get me out of here.

Acous. Gtr.

Elec. Gtr. 3

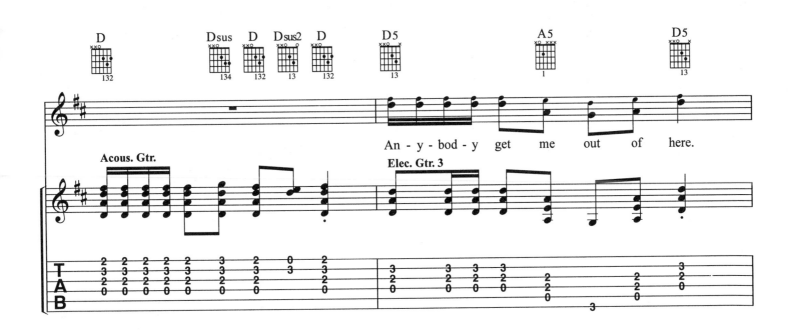

An - y - bod - y get me out of here.

Acous. Gtr.

Elec. Gtr. 3

III. Nobody Likes You (4:03)

Words by MIKE DIRNT
Music by GREEN DAY

Bright waltz ♩. = 76

Intro:

Cont. rhy. simile

Bells

Verse:

D   D/A   D/G   D/A

I   fell   a - sleep   while   watch - ing   Spike   T   V   af - ter

*Elec. Gtr. plays D chord while bass changes root notes throughout.

D   D/A   D/G   D/A

ten   cups   of   cof - fee   and   you're   still   not   here.

IV. Rock and Roll Girlfriend (5:20)
Moderately fast ♩ = 172

Words by TRE COOL
Music by GREEN DAY

V. We're Coming Home Again (6:06)

Words by BILLIE JOE
Music by GREEN DAY

Slower ♩ = 144

Intro:

108

110

112

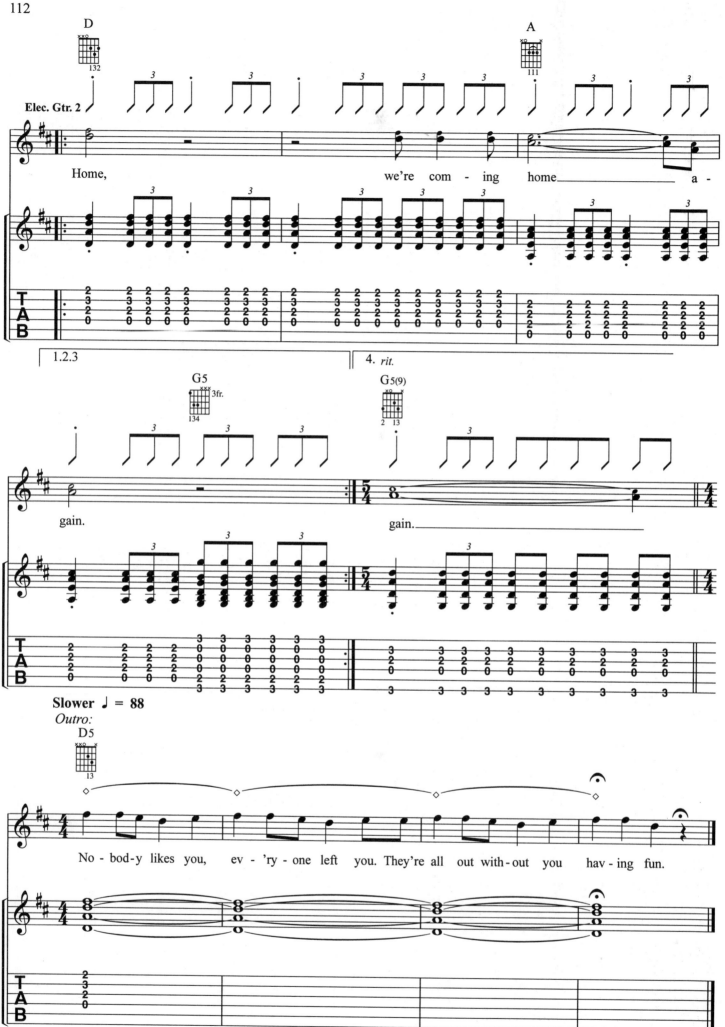

WHATSERNAME

Words by BILLIE JOE
Music by GREEN DAY

All gtrs. in Drop D: ⑥ = D

116

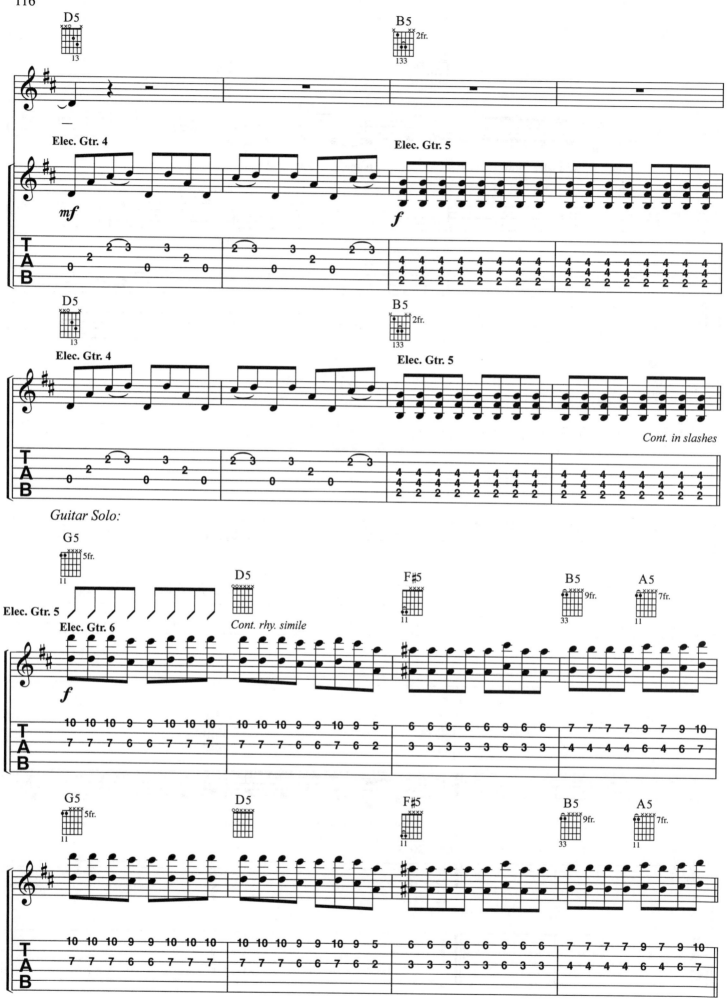

Whatsername - 7 - 4
PGM0423

Bridge 1:

Interlude:

w/Rhy. Fig. 1 *(Elec. Gtr. 4) 3 times*

GUITAR TAB GLOSSARY **

TABLATURE EXPLANATION

READING TABLATURE: Tablature illustrates the six strings of the guitar. Notes and chords are indicated by the placement of fret numbers on a given string(s).

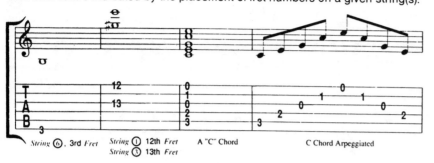

String ⑥, 3rd Fret   String ① 12th Fret   A "C" Chord   C Chord Arpeggiated
String ③ 13th Fret

BENDING NOTES

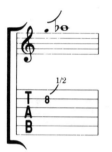

HALF STEP: Play the note and bend string one half step.*

PREBEND AND RELEASE: Bend the string, play it, then release to the original note.

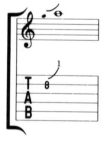

WHOLE STEP: Play the note and bend string one whole step.

RHYTHM SLASHES

STRUM INDICA-TIONS: Strum with indicated rhythm.

The chord voicings are found on the first page of the transcription underneath the song title.

INDICATING SINGLE NOTES USING RHYTHM SLASHES: Very often single notes are incorporated into a rhythm part. The note name is indicated above the rhythm slash with a fret number and a string indication.

*A half step is the smallest interval in Western music; it is equal to one fret. A whole step equals two frets.

**By Kenn Chipkin and Aaron Stang

ARTICULATIONS

HAMMER ON: Play lower note, then "hammer on" to higher note with another finger. Only the first note is attacked.

PULL OFF: Play higher note, then "pull off" to lower note with another finger. Only the first note is attacked.

LEGATO SLIDE: Play note and slide to the following note. (Only first note is attacked).

PALM MUTE: The note or notes are muted by the palm of the pick hand by lightly touching the string(s) near the bridge.

ACCENT: Notes or chords are to be played with added emphasis.

DOWN STROKES AND UPSTROKES: Notes or chords are to be played with either a downstroke (⊓) or upstroke (∨) of the pick.